Discover
today and

First published in the UK in 2002 by
Select All
Glan Y Wern
Park Road
Barmouth
LL42 1PH

ISBN 0-9541128-1-4

A CIP catalogue record of this book is available from the British Library.

Every effort has been made to ensure the information contained in this publication is accurate at the time of going to press. Select All cannot be held responsible for any inaccuracies.

Information in this book is for guidance only.

Introduction and Acknowledgements

Thank you for buying 'Discover Barmouth'. We hope you find it an informative and enjoyable book. We considered the idea of publishing some form of guide to Barmouth town and its history a number of years ago. It grew into a more interesting proposition when a friend, who runs the local newsagents, complained about not having any publication to offer curious visitors. However, as the authors of the book, we would like to point out that we are not qualified historians or researchers...just interested locals. The book does not pretend to be definitive in any form. The main criteria for inclusion of information has been whether we considered it of relevance and interest. It has been an immense joy researching and putting it together, and we welcome any contribution, positive or otherwise, that will help us to make the next edition of 'Discover Barmouth' a more informative read.

This first edition would not have made it to the presses without the help and encouragement of Mrs. Karen Owen regarding Barmouth Bridge, Mrs. B. Morris for permission to reproduce her photographs, Mr. Gwynfor Owen for photographs and information, Valerie and Kevin McArdell of Oriel Gallery for the restoration of numerous old photographs and Mr. Gordon Walters for his detailed library of cuttings regarding Barmy. We are also indebted to Gwynedd Archive Services for their assistance, Mr. Gussy Morris for his enthusiasm and his imaging skills, Mr. Tony Isles regarding Ty Gwyn and Mr. Colin Allday, coxswain of Moira Barrie, and Mr. John Probert, Secretary of Barmouth RNLI, for information regarding Barmouth's lifeboats. We are also grateful to Owena's late Nain, Mrs. Jennie Owen, for keeping a library of cuttings and photographs about the local area. We would also like to place on record our thanks to all those who help maintain the town's places of worship, the staff at Barmouth Library, particularly Liz Speake, for their assistance and knowledge and, most importantly, Mrs. Maureen Owen for encouragement, proof reading and grammar lessons. Oh... and thanks to Jon Vine and Mai Wadsworth for nurturing the idea, and suffering a six-mile hike in the name of research. Finally, an obvious, but heartfelt thank you to our family and friends for their patience and encouragement.

Regards
Owena and John

Contents

List of Illustrations

We are grateful to the following for allowing us to reproduce their photographs;

Bibliography

The following publications have been used during the research of this book:

Austin, Stephen - From the Footplate Cambrian Coast Express - 1992.
Anderson, J.R.L - High Mountain & Cold Seas - A biography of H.W Tilman - 1980.
Blacks Picturesque Guide to Wales - 1866.
Evans - Tour Through North Wales - 1798.
Jones, E.Rosalie - A History of Barmouth and its Vicinity - 1909.
Lewis's Topographical Dictionary of Wales.
Lewis, E.A - Welsh Port Books - 1550-1603.
Lloyd, Lewis - Sails on the Mawddach - 1981.
Lloyd, Lewis - Wherever Freights May Offer - 1993.
Lloyd, Lewis - Cymru a'r mor/Maritime Wales page 109-122
Hambly Mark, Bodlander Adrian, Southern Dave - Llangollen Railway Society - Railways of the Wnion Valley and the Mawddach Estuary - 1991.
Morris, Jeff - The Story of the Barmouth Lifeboats - 1992.
Owen, H.J - Treasures of the Mawddach - 1950.
O'Connor, Bernard - The History of Mawddach Crescent Felga Fawr, Arthog, North Wales - 2000.
The Barmouth Publicity Association - Explore Barmouth Places in and Around the Town.

Articles
Journal of the Meirioneth Historical and Record society - vol. xII 1994 part 1, pp 43-50 - 'Mr Jelf's Proprietary Chapel at a Welsh Watering Place' by Roger L.Brown.
Journal of the Merioneth Historical and Record society - vol. III page 33, - 'Caerdeon Chapel' by H.J.Owen.

Chapter 1

From Port to Resort

The seaside town of Barmouth nestles beside a mountain, at the mouth of the Mawddach estuary, as it empties into Cardigan Bay. The estuary provides the town with its original Welsh name of Abermawddach - Aber meaning the mouth of an estuary. Various other versions of the name include Abermaw and Bermo. The English name of Barmouth is thought to have been corrupted from A(bermaw)ddach.

Towards the end of the 18th century, the town became an important port due to the shipbuilding activity on the estuary and the town's central position in Cardigan Bay. Prior to this though, there are few records for the area.

1565 – Concerned that the Welsh coast was rife with pirates, Queen Elizabeth I commissioned a survey of the 'creeks and ports' of the county of Meirioneth in this year. Barmouth was recorded as having 4 houses and 2 ferries. With no actual seagoing vessels of its own at the time, the ferries probably did some inshore fishing, as herring is documented as the staple diet of the locals.

1587 – 'L'Angel de Bermo', the first recorded ship to be Barmouth owned, was importing much needed wheat, barley, pilcorn (the naked oat) and rye into the area for local use.

18th century – The Welsh woollen industry became well established in this century, with Meirioneth being one of the leading counties. Much of the activity was focused around Dolgellau, the Mawddach estuary and Barmouth. The main product of the local inhabitants' efforts were 'webs', long lengths of coarse white cloth produced from wool and cotton. This industry remained largely cottage in nature, with most families owning their own loom. The head of the household could, in an effort to support his family, spend up to fourteen hours a day on the machine.

The majority of the webs produced in Dolgellau were taken overland, to be sold on by the Shrewsbury Drapers' Company. Barmouth meanwhile, was producing webs from good quality lambs' wool. A healthy export

Mawddach River Lighter Boat which was used to carry goods for export down the estuary to Barmouth

trade began to the slave owners of South America, the West Indies and the southern states of North America. The webs were used to clothe the slaves. Barmouth and Dolgellau had found an effective combination for the local industries of farming and shipping.

1770 to 1790 – With ample availability of quality oak in the vicinity and along the Mawddach estuary, shipbuilding became an important contributor to the local economy in this period, with around 140 vessels being built on the estuary. Most were constructed at Maes-Y-Garnedd, near Llanelltyd, but there were other shipbuilding yards, including Penmanepool and Llanelltyd Bridge. Once the boat structures were complete, they were towed or floated downstream to Barmouth, to be fitted out at one of the three shipyards on the harbour.

1775 to 1783 – The American War of Independence had a dramatic and negative effect on the Meirioneth trade of wool and 'webs'. To compound matters, Barmouth also lost a number of locally registered vessels in the conflict. Also, Dolgellau began to suffer in its trade with Shrewsbury, as it fought to compete with the large steam powered mills based in Northern England.

1793 – The Napoleonic War worsened the already declining Meirioneth wool trade. The conflict with France eventually saw the complete cessation of wool exports from Barmouth by sea. In **1798**, a Mr. Evans wrote a book called a "Tour through North Wales". In it he describes a family he meets in Barmouth, and the poverty in which they live:
"As I further ascended the hill, a hut, little better than the cote *(a place for animals)* I had left, forbade my approach. At the entrance, for door there was none, stood a tall female figure, which from her tattered dress and sallow countenance, you would scarcely have supposed to have been human; with a distorted figure at her breast. I spoke, but she, not understanding my language, and little supposing I would enter such a dwelling, still kept her post. I then took the child and pointed for admittance. The hut consisted of one room upon the ground floor, divided by a partition of lath and reeds. The floor was the native soil, rendered very hard and uneven from long and unequal pressure. At the farther end was a fire of turf, laid upon a few stones, near which stood a three legged stool, a small

cast-iron pot, some branches of broom tied up for a besom *(a brush)*, and a few bundles of rushes thrown down for a bed. This constituted the principle furniture! At the other end was a lank meagre figure sitting at a loom, weaving coarse linen; the father of the family.

"At this employment, after fourteen hours' toil, he could earn 8-pence. But a chronic illness, occasioned by low debilitating diet, prevents his following so close as constantly to earn this. A similar cause prevented the wife from properly looking after four sickly children. The eldest was stinted in its growth; the second lame; the third blind; and the youngest, though two years old, still at the breast and wasting away with the tabes dorsalis *(a chronic degenerative disease of the nervous system)."*

1795 – On the site of an older inn, the Cors-Y-Gedol Arms was built to provide accommodation for the growing number of travellers visiting the area. Sea bathing, which began in 1760, was increasing in popularity. This imposing hotel still stands today on the high street, not far from Wool-worth. Note the sign that proclaims its establishment in 1700!

1797 – A private bill to deepen Barmouth harbour was forced through parliament. The bill was funded by an impressive collection of around 200 local 'worthies', including small freeholders, manufacturers and shop-keepers, tradesmen and master mariners. They wanted to make it safer and easier to enter the harbour and to develop a new quay. The work was eventually completed in **1802** at a total cost of £1660.00, equivalent to around £75,000 in today's money.

1798 – Bathing machines were introduced onto Barmouth beach. They allowed modest 'ladies' to bathe in the open sea. However, the occupant would have to sit in the static machine and wait for the tide to wash in…and then out. Eventually, horse drawn models superseded these fixed machines. Sea bathing was not only fashionable amongst the wealthy, but considered very beneficial and therapeutic. Many infirm individuals visited Barmouth for this reason. Sufferers of scurvy also visited the town to obtain the 'scurvy grass', a plentiful herb growing along the banks of the Mawddach estuary.

Circa 1798 – The road we know today, along the banks of the estuary, from Bontddu to Barmouth, was finally blasted through the rock in around this year. Prior to this, the main route into Barmouth from the east was over the mountains, via Cae Gyronwy. The traveller would either continue across the hills directly to Dyffryn, or drop down via Panorama Walk, to enter Barmouth close to where Porkington Terrace is situated today. Alternative routes into other parts of the town evolved over the years. One example brought the traveller down into the maze of old cottages known as Hen Bermo (*old Barmouth and locally known as The Rock*).

Circa 1800 – Barmouth shipping began to benefit from the increasingly active slate trade as Blaenau Ffestiniog mines and their infrastructure developed. Barmouth ships would collect slate from the Dwyryd and Glaslyn estuaries, some ten miles up the coast, and transport the cargo to London and other ports, including a number in Ireland.

Circa 1829 – When the foundations of the present day Lion Hotel in Barmouth High Street were being laid, the remains of an old quay were found, including several ancient anchors and iron rings. This suggests that, at some point in the past, boats were being moored as far inland as this part of the town. Also, at a later date, when the drains were being cut along the high street, the remains of an old boat were found.

1839 – Ynys-Y-Brawd, or Friar's Island, is the small piece of land at the end of the causeway that stretches in front of the Bath House. At one time it could only be reached at low tide. Today, however, a concrete walkway links it to the main promenade. Two attempts have been made to build a lighthouse on the island. The first attempt, in 1839, saw the construction of a large four-sided block, which was around 22 feet above high-water mark. Unfortunately, a raging storm destroyed it. Undaunted, the authorities began work on a round tower with a square base in 1843. The construction had reached the height of fifteen feet when another storm removed all trace of it. Today, a simple pole with a red flashing light stands on the site.

Circa 1840 – The imports into Barmouth harbour became much more varied than the exports of oak timber and bark, and farm produce. Imports included flour, tea, coffee, sugar, candles, beans, peas, oatmeal, bricks, tin, lead, pitch and some timber for house and shipbuilding.

Barmouth to Dolgellau Road near Glandwr

Once in the harbour the goods would be transferred to smaller boats, which would convey them to various locations along Mawddach estuary, including Glandwr, Penmaenpool, Maes Y Garnedd and Llanelltyd Bridge. Men with carts would then take the items inland for distribution to shopkeepers, innkeepers and tradesmen.

Glandwr is a little tributary about 2 miles up the estuary from Barmouth. Many boats would come to this area carrying items such as seaweed, which was used by the local farmers as a type of manure. Wheat was also brought for processing into flour at Glandwr Mill.

Today, the tributary has been cut off for use by boats, by the main road from Dolgellau to Barmouth. The Mill can still be seen though, on the right hand side of the road when travelling towards Barmouth.

1865 – The Aberystwyth and Welsh Coast Railway arrived at Fairbourne, on the southern side of Mawddach estuary. Passengers bound for Barmouth had to complete their journey by ferry. Black's Picturesque Guide to Wales, written in **1866**, provides us with an insight into this arduous final stage; "There are two miles to drive in an open car, followed by a walk from 50 to 300 or 400 yards, according to the state of the tide, over the rough pebbly beach, to reach the small boat, which has only one man to manage it. The sail is often very rough, and nearly half-a-mile in length. If it is low water, there is a bar of rough gravel (perhaps 300 yards long) in the centre of the estuary, over which it is necessary to walk, and then another boat has to be taken to reach Barmouth – a mode of proceeding not very convenient for ladies and children."

1867 – On 3rd June, Barmouth viaduct was opened to horse drawn traffic. Locomotive trains began service in October, completing the railway link from Ruabon, through Dolgellau, to Barmouth. The arrival of the train had a dramatic effect on the estuary's river trade. Even though the Welsh Railway Company was compelled to include a swing section in the viaduct, to allow tall boats to continue to sail unhindered along the estuary, the shipbuilding and local maritime industries suffered greatly from the arrival of the train. Local merchants and manufacturers soon found the railways to be a faster and more versatile method of transporting their goods. In **1867**, over 150 vessels entered and left Barmouth harbour. By **1876**, the number had dropped to less than a dozen.

Barmouth Bridge, c1890, prior to the construction of the swing section

1870s - The railway also brought more visitors to the town. New buildings were constructed to meet their demands. Marine Parade, which today runs parallel with the promenade, and still mainly consists of hotels and guesthouses, was completed in this period. Porkington Terrace, which overlooks Barmouth viaduct, was also built during these years.

Many shops were also constructed on the sand streets below 'Hen Bermo'. Some of the present day shops and offices along the high street still have sand below the slate floors in their cellars.

1879 – Six miles downstream from Barmouth, along the Mawddach, is Penmaenpool. A natural inlet in the turn of the estuary, it was used to deliver goods and merchandise to local merchants. The shipbuilder's yards of Maes-Y-Garnedd were even further downstream. When The Penmaenpool Bridge Company Ltd proposed a bridge to span the estuary, there was great opposition from both merchants and shipbuilders. Despite the fact that shipbuilding on Mawddach estuary was in terminal decline, the company, in an effort to placate their objectors, agreed to include in their plans, a 30-foot draw bridge section in the centre of the bridge, to allow the passage of tall ships. It was, however, on condition of a revival in the shipbuilding trade. It never occurred, so the section was not included in the completed bridge, which was opened in this year.

In the early days, the main traffic across the bridge would have been horse drawn carts or foot passengers. Many workers from the gold mines of Bontddu on the northern side of the estuary, lived in the Penmanpool area, on the southern side.

1881 – According to the Parish of Llanaber, the Barmouth population had increased to 2,155 in this year. In **1801** it was recorded as 463. In eighty years the population had more than quadrupled!

1920 – In July of this year, electric lighting arrived at the town. Prior to this, the town had been lit by gas since 1862.

1923 – Barmouth is hit by a severe storm, which causes extensive damage to the sea wall and promenade, portions of which collapse. Several buildings on the front are left vulnerable and in serious danger.

1930 – Work began to construct new sea-defences and a promenade for the town. The scheme included the construction of 46 timber groynes and a sea wall measuring 7200 feet in length, which included a reinforced concrete promenade and a 'carriage drive'. In November 1931, mid way through construction, a high tide, backed by a south-westerly gale destroyed over 690 feet of the partly completed wall.

1933 – Eventually, after 3 years work the sea-defences and promenade were completed and were officially opened by Lloyd George on September 22nd. The final bill for the project was £170,000. Despite alleged financial assurances from central government, Barmouth Urban Council footed most of the bill. It nearly bankrupted the town.

1943 – In the Barmouth vicinity during the war years, The Royal Marines Training Group conducted seamanship training for troops. By the banks of the estuary, at the southern end of Barmouth Bridge, stands a red brick terrace of around eight four-storey houses, called Mawddach Crescent. At short notice The War Office requisitioned the houses, and most families were required to leave, apart from some who, due to ill health, were allowed

Barmouth Bathing Machines c1910

to stay in a few ground floor rooms. The Royal Marines moved into the remainder of the floors, and even knocked doors through the adjoining walls on the second floor to allow access from one end of the terrace to the other.

1966 – Following the publication in 1963 of Dr. Richard Beeching's report on the state of Britain's railways, various branch lines and around 2,000 stations were closed around the country. One of the causalities was the line from Ruabon, through Dolgellau to Barmouth.

In the same year a tragic accident occurred when a pleasure craft from Barmouth, collided with Penamenpool bridge and sank with the loss of fifteen lives.

1972 – A concrete walkway to link the promenade with Ynys Y Brawd is built, thereby forcing the tide to enter Barmouth harbour to the south of the former island. Many local fishermen and yachtspeople feel that it was the completion of the walkway that led to the silting up of the harbour. Today, during low tides, it is virtually impossible to cross by boat from one side of the harbour to the other, due to the sandbanks.

1999 - Barmouth's beach is awarded the European Blue Flag. The award is given to beaches that meet strict criteria on water quality, safety, beach cleanliness, dog control, disabled access, etc.

Chapter 2
Places of Interest

Ty Gwyn and the Maritime Exhibition

Ty Gwyn was one of the four houses recorded in a survey of Creeks and Ports commissioned by Queen Elizabeth I in 1565. Built by the Vaughan family, of Cors-Y-Gedol hall near Dyffryn, in around 1470, it was designed to be a safe house for communications with the Earl of Pembroke, Jasper Tudor, and his nephew, the future Henry VII. They were planning an invasion of England and Ty Gwyn's location was more suitable than Cors Y Gedol, should they suddenly need to escape via the sea.

The building still stands, but, as it is now a café, the only planning done these days is for tomorrow's lunch menu. More appropriately however, the upper floor of the building houses a maritime exhibition. Opened in around 1999, it features historical articles and photographs of Barmouth as a port and the historical background to the building itself. Open daily from May to October, entry is free, but donations are welcomed and used to maintain the facility.

In the late 1970s, divers from Glaslyn Aqua Club found the wrecks of two ships - one on top of another - just off the coast of the village of Dyffryn Ardudwy, 5 miles north of Barmouth. Researchers believe that the boats foundered 200 years apart on the notorious St. Patrick's causeway. Divers have recovered a bronze bell of a ship, dated 1677, from one of the wrecks. The ship was also carrying a cargo of pure white marble, which is thought to have originated from the Cararra quarries in Northern Italy. The organisers of Ty Gwyn would like to create a permanent facility in their museum to display the various artefacts from the wrecks and, therefore, make them available to the public. Firstly, however, thousands of pounds must be raised in order to pay for the restoration work, etc. Any size donation will help the committee towards their aim.

The Bath House

This proud and imposing building stands on the edge of the water as you round the corner from the harbour. In fact, the pillars of the balcony regularly stand in the sea during moderate to high tides. Being four stories high and the only building on the seaward side of the promenade, it naturally

Ty Gwyn and Old Barmouth from the Harbour, c1865. Note the absence of the railway bridge.

draws your attention when viewed from the beach or Old Barmouth.

The precise history of the building is elusive. Some individuals say it was used to wash slaves prior to their transportation to the Americas. However, we do know that it in 1840 William Barnett owned it. He was also the owner of the Cors-Y-Gedol Arms. At that time, the Bath House was a far less impressive building, consisting of only two stories. However, it housed a large lead lined bath, which was used to provide visitors and locals with 'beneficial sea baths', which could be taken hot or cold. When the lead bath was sold, the proceeds were used to extend the building to its present day heights. William Barnett was also responsible for replacing the fixed bathing machines with the horse drawn variety.

The Sailor's Institute

This building is probably one of the last remaining examples of its kind in Wales. Constructed in 1890 of corrugated iron, it is located on the harbour beside the railway bridge. Originally, it was designed as a Christian haven for local and visiting sailors.

In 1984, following renovation work, the institute received a Prince of Wales Award for preserving the original interior and maintaining the exterior.

The institute is open daily from 10am. Entrance is free, but donations are gratefully received, and visitors are welcome to browse through the selection of local and national newspapers, and the boating and yachting periodicals. There is also a small presentation of photographs and articles comparing the Barmouth of today and yesteryear, and a recreation room housing a billiards table.

The Round House

Barmouth Round House is situated near the harbour, behind Ty Gwyn. As the name implies, it is a circular building, with an internal diameter of around sixteen feet. The stone walls are two feet thick and the pitched roof is covered in slates. Although there is what looks like a chimney at the peak of the roof, there are no fireplaces or ventilation ducts. The chimney serves only for decoration.

On the 21st October 1830, the freeholders and principals of the town held a meeting at the Cors-Y-Gedol Arms. They were concerned that, as Barmouth became a busier seaport with an ever increasing number of visiting ships and their crews, more and more incidents of disorderly behaviour were occurring. By the end of the meeting they had decided to build the Round House in which any drunkards could be detained until they were sober and the local court was sitting.

The building was eventually completed in 1834. It consisted of two individual cells – one for women and one for men – with an external door to each. The rooms also had an opening at roof level, which was secured by iron bars, and provided natural light and ventilation.

The building served its purpose well until 1861, when the opening of a police station in the town left it with no precise purpose. The structure gradually fell into disrepair. In 1939, Barmouth Town Council considered demolishing it, in favour of a housing scheme. And, in the 1950s, people who lived on the harbour, including the author's 'hen nain' (grandmother), used one cell as a coal store!

Eventually, the local community and council realised the wisdom of preserving the town's heritage. In the 1980s, the Round House was renovated and the area around it landscaped. Today, it is a must for any visitor interested in Barmouth's history. For authenticity, the building even houses a couple of drunks in the summertime.

Barmouth Bridge

When the Aberystwyth and Welsh Coast Railway arrived at Fairbourne in 1865, it was only a matter of time before the railway and its benefits should make the relatively short hop over the estuary.

Soon, work to bridge the estuary was started by the engineer Benjamin Piercy and the Cleveland Bridge and Engineering Co Ltd, a Darlington contractor. The bridge was to consist of 113 timber spans and an eight span iron section. Each of the iron columns supporting the structure was around eight feet in diameter and had to sink 120 feet below sea level to find the rock floor. Also incorporated into the iron section was a rolling 'cock-and-draw', or 'over-draw' section, which could be opened to allow tall sailing ships to continue up the estuary.

On 3rd June 1867, the bridge was opened to horse drawn carriages. Locomotive services began in October of the same year. On 28 July 1900, the 'cock-and-draw' section was opened for the last time. It was replaced by the steel swinging span which we see today, and once again, construction was done by Cleveland Bridge and Engineering Co Ltd.

In 1980, divers discovered that the glamorous sounding Teredo Navalis shipworm had bored into 69 timber piles. The larvae lived in the wood and caused holes several feet in length. The bridge was closed to locomotive traffic on the 13th October whilst a £1.8 million programme of repairs was completed. Eventually, after an absence of over five and a half years, the bridge was fully reopened to locomotive trains in April 1986.

Today, the bridge is one of the largest surviving timber viaducts in Britain, and stretches 2,292 feet across the estuary (almost half a mile). Following the complete cessation of travel by tall ships along the estuary, the swing section of the bridge is rarely opened. The most recent examples were in March 1984 and April 1987. Both occasions were for test purposes.

Test opening of the swing section of Barmouth Bridge in 1965

St Marys Church - Llanaber

This Medieval church is located on the A496 towards Harlech, about 1.5 miles north of Barmouth. A Church has existed on the site for approximately 1400 years. The present example was built by Hywel ap Gruffudd ap Cynan, a great grandson of Owain Gwynedd, who became overlord of this part of Meirionnydd in 1202, but was dead by 1216. The first recorded rector of the parish was William de la Pole in 1383.

Allegedly, the original intention was to site the church in a field near Sylfaen Farm, on the hills above the Mawddach estuary, and workmen began laying the foundations of stone and timber. However, when they returned the following morning their work had been destroyed. Puzzled as to what or who would have done such a thing, they set about making repairs. However, once again, the foundations were demolished during the night. Rumours of ghosts and evil spirits spread amongst the workmen, but eventually a small group of sturdy, if not nervous, men agreed to keep watch on the sight through the night. At some point during their vigil, the men claimed that the foundations were ripped apart by some unseen force, and as they

fled in terror, voices could be heard crying "Llanaber! Llanaber!" The next day, the men concluded that the site of the church should be Llanaber, and not Sylfaen. And so began the arduous task of moving the stone and timber overland the four-mile distance to its new home. Supposedly, to this day, there are still upright stones to be seen in the field where the demolition of the first foundations are said to have occurred.

Although today's Barmouth town has the largest population, the proper title of the parish is 'Llanaber, with Barmouth, Caerdeon and Bontddu'. Llanaber Church was the first for the Parish. Idyllically located on a hill overlooking Cardigan Bay, it is the finest 13th-century church in Gwynedd. The main entrance, via the South door, is reputed to be one of the finest examples of early English architecture in the country. The nave, or the central hall of the church, is divided on either side into five arcades, with massive piers, or pillars, which are Norman in character. The Chancel, at the eastern end of the church is the oldest part. The roof timbers are thought to date from the 16th century, as are the timbers in the Nave. The four Clerestory windows on either side of the Nave are delightful examples of early English Lancets, i.e. narrow pointed windows.

As you enter the church, located in the north west corner are two ancient stones dating from the 5th century. They are probably amongst the earliest Christian memorials in the country. The first stone was formerly used in the locality as a footbridge, but was placed in the church in the 19th century. The second was found on the beach, not far from the church. Both stones have simple inscriptions in Roman capitals that read horizontally.

At one point in history, there was a public house near to or adjoining Llanaber Church, and the cellar of the hostelry supposedly provided a safe storehouse for smugglers. The focus of the smugglers' efforts was often kegs of spirits and part of the cargoes of the vessels wrecked on the Barmouth coast.

In the cemetery, there are many examples of 'Cistfaen' – which translates to English as 'Table Tomb'. These box like tombs cover the graves and are made from stone to a height of 2 or 3 feet above ground level. Being hollow, they provided a convenient location for smugglers to store their illicit cargo.

St. Davids Church

As the amount of trade passing through Barmouth harbour increased in the early 1800s, so the population of the town grew. Eventually, the original Church of St. Mary's in Llanaber, became too small for the needs of the Parish. In 1830 St. David's Church, or Eglwys Dewi Sant to use its Welsh name, was erected. It was built near the harbour on the site of a former shipbuilding yard. In fact the site was so close to the harbour and the sea, there was concern that sand drifts could make access difficult. And for some years after completion, the critic's fears were proven, as the sand drifts became a regular cause of annoyance for the worshippers. Until St. John's was completed in 1892, St. David's held English services in the morning and Welsh services in the evening. After 1892, St. David's was host to only Welsh services.

The Church remains a prominent feature on the landscape of the harbour, and is still in use today. Compared to St. Mary's and St. John's, the crucifix shaped interior of St. David's is relatively plain. However, the simplicity of the interior adds more impetus to the impressive copies of eight Raphael cartoons that adorn the whitewashed walls and were donated to the Church by Lady Russon of Glan-Y-Mawddach. A cartoon is a design for tapestries. The originals, which are housed in the Victoria and Albert Museum, depict a variety of scenes and were used by Flemish weavers to create a series of tapestries for the Sistine Chapel in the Vatican.

St. Philips Church - Caerdeon

In the 1850s there was little or no provision in the Parish of Llanaber for worship in English, even though Barmouth was developing as a watering place for more and more English families.

In 1859, The Reverend William Edward Jelf, a former student of Oxford, moved to live in Caerdeon, approximately half way between Barmouth and Bontddu. Due to the lack of availability of English services, he started holding private Anglican services in his home for his family, pupils and staff. Soon, however, a congregation began to gather in his home and so, in 1862, he decided to build a private Church in his grounds. It was not long before a war of words (and paper) broke out between;

- the Parish rector, Revd John Jones, who disliked Reverend Jelf and was against the English services. However. he had no room or

The Circus passes St. Davids Church in 1885

inclination to begin English services himself;

- his superior, Bishop James Colquhoun Campbell of Bangor, who had mistakenly licensed Caerdeon Church;
- and Reverend Jelf who was technically in breach of ecclesiastical law.

Eventually, Jelf lost his case at the Court of Arches in London. No doubt embarrassed by his error, and wary of the negative repercussions upon the local Church following the case, Bishop Campbell sought to avoid a recurrence of the incident by supporting a new parliamentary bill. It would allow Bishops in Wales to licence a Church for English worship if there were ten or more prospective worshippers in the town who were prepared to provide a building and meet all the associated costs.

Caerdeon House and the Church soon passed into the hands of Mr. Samuel Holland M.P., and in 1887 the Parish of Caerdeon with Bontddu was established, and the Church was consecrated.

Just as Reverend Jelf did not conform with Welsh society of 1860, so the design of his Church does not conform with its location. Modelled on the features from an Italian hillside Chapel in the Southern Alps and the striking architecture of Basque Churches in South West France, it was designed by Reverend Jelf's brother-in-law. The results are a simple rectangular shape, plain windows and local tiles, giving it an almost barn like appearance. Located just off the main road to Dolgellau, about four miles from Barmouth, the Church is hidden from passing traffic by a canopy of trees. Some of its more notable features include an interesting bell-turret housing a carillon of four bells, which spans the chancel arch. There is also a chimney that was an outlet for the fire built underneath the chancel floor, and used as an early form of heating.

It is worth locating and visiting this hidden Church if only to view the structure of the building. Why not see if your friends pass any comment when you slip a photograph of it in the middle of your snaps from Tuscany?

St. Johns Church

Dominating the landscape and keeping watch over the town

of Barmouth is the Church of St John the Divine, claimed to be one of the finest ecclesiastical structures in Wales. However, the story surrounding its construction is colourful.

Following the completion of the Church of St. David on Barmouth harbour in 1830, successive rectors contemplated the idea of a larger and more magnificent edifice for the town. The appointment of Reverend Edward Hughes to the town in 1887 was one the most important steps in making St. Johns Church a reality. He found that St. David's was inadequate for the size of the congregations wishing to attend an Anglican service. Despite increasing the number of services, more clergy help and improved seating, the only viable option in the long term was to build a larger Church.

Tentative initial plans were completed, only for the originators of the idea to realise that they needed to raise in excess of £18,000 (equivalent to £1,160,000 in 2002) for the project to be completed. Step forward, Mrs. Dyson Perrins of Malvern, friend of Fanny Talbot *(see page 30)*, and a member of the Lea & Perrins (Worcestershire sauce) dynasty. A lady of great wealth and sympathy for the Church, she happened to be living at Plas Mynach, her Barmouth holiday home, when she heard of the local Church's project. She and her family were delighted to help, and subscribed £15,000 (over £950,000 in today's money) to the total cost of the project. And so, on August 28 1889, HRH Princess Beatrice, daughter of Queen Victoria, laid the foundation stone for the edifice. In a cavity below the stone was also placed a bottle containing a copy of 'The Times', 'Church Times', 'North Wales Chronicle', 'Cambrian News', 'Barmouth Advertiser', 'The Llan', 'The Oswestry Advertiser', and a copy of 'The Wild Flowers of Barmouth'.

Building work continued at a steady pace over the next 20 months. Work was nearing completion when, early one Saturday morning in September 1891, the massive 100 foot tower suddenly collapsed into the chancel, demolishing three quarters of the north wall and part of the gable end of the south side. At the time, it was rumoured that the shelf of the cliff, on which the foundations had been laid, was too narrow. The architect however, attributed the collapse to recent blasting operations in the area surrounding the Church, in an effort to provide it with more light.

Following such a dramatic disaster to an already costly project, there was concern over whether the edifice could be completed. Mrs. Dyson, however, once again came to the financial rescue, and the tower, with its clock, was rebuilt in time for the consecration of the Church by the Bishop of Bangor in 1895.

The interior of the Church is as impressive as the outside. Just inside the entrance, below the west window, is the Angel Statue Font. Carved in Inverness from a huge block of white marble. The stone was originally quarried at Carrara in Italy, transported on a wagon by a team of oxen to the port of Avenza-Marina and shipped to Britain. Other interesting features include a mosaic floor in the Chancel, choir stalls of richly carved oak and a lectern of wrought iron and copper representing the Sower and the Seed.

St John's collapsed tower, 1891

Chapter 4
People of Interest

John Ruskin (1819 – 1900)

Born in London, the son of a prosperous wine merchant, Ruskin became the greatest British art critic and social commentator of the Victorian Age. His ideas inspired the Arts and Crafts Movement and the founding of the National Trust, the Society for the Protection of Ancient Buildings and the Labour Movement. He fiercely attacked the worst aspects of industrialisation, and actively promoted art education and museums for the working classes. He was also an accomplished artist, scientist, poet, environmentalist, and philosopher.

As a social commentator, Ruskin was keen to experiment, and one of his ideas was to try and create a Utopian society. With this aim in mind, he created the Guild of St. George. One of his closest friends was the philanthropist, Fanny Talbot *(see page 30)*, who lived in Barmouth. She donated some land and cottages to Ruskin's Guild, and so began his project in 1875.

Ruskin's Cottages, as they came to be known, soon became one of his more successful experiments. In total, there were 13 cottages, dotted across the hill of Hen Bermo. Some of the principles of the venture were that;

- the rents on the properties should never be increased, but payments should be made promptly by the tenants
- the tenants would not be accepted unless they were of good character
- any improvement that could add to the cottagers comfort be carried out
- each tenant should be helped in sickness or if in any difficulty
- tea and cake should be provided on February 8, to help celebrate Ruskin's birthday.

Ruskin was only able to visit his experiment once, in the summer of 1876. He met many of his tenants during that visit, including M. August Guyard *(see page 30)*, a Frenchman with very similar ideals as his himself.

Periodic bouts of ill health over the following years, including mental illness, prevented Ruskin from further developing his Utopian experiment. In 1884 he retired to Coniston in the Lake District. After 1889 he stopped writing and rarely spoke in public. He died of influenza in 1900.

Fanny Talbot (1824 – 1917)

Mrs. Talbot was a philanthropist and one of Barmouth's most generous and influential inhabitants. She lived in Tyn-Y-Ffynon *(see page 50)*, which was a large house at the top of Hen Bermo, looking out over the harbour.

In 1875, she presented land and 13 cottages in Barmouth to John Ruskin, and became patron of his Guild of St. George. Ruskin used the cottages to explore his social theory of creating a Utopian society via a housing co-operative. Although a minor success, she became frustrated with Ruskin when he only visited the project on one occasion. Mrs. Talbot was left to manage the day to day running of the properties and their tenants.

In March 1895, she donated 4.5 acres of land, which was alongside her house, to the National Trust. Her friends Canon Hardwicke Drummond Rawnsley, and Miss Octavia Hill, a social reformer and one of Ruskin's pupils, had only recently formed the trust, with Sir Robert Hunter, a lawyer. Their aim was to preserve places of natural beauty and historic interest for the nation. Mrs. Talbot's donation became the National Trust's first property and is known as Dinas Oleu, or, in English, The Fortress of Light.

In the 1890s the authoress and feminist, Miss Frances Cobbe, offered to bequeath her large and valuable collection of books and manuscripts to the town, if a suitable building could be provided to house them. Once again, Mrs. Talbot was one of the first to generously step forward and contribute to the appeal, which was launched by the library committee. She gave £400, which amounted to just under a third of the total sum required.

In 1961, her former imposing home, Tyn-Y-Ffynnon, was destroyed by fire. Today, a two storey cream house stands on the sought after spot. Plaques on the boundary wall of the property commemorate the former occupant's generosity to the local community.

Auguste Guyard (? – 1883)

M. Guyard was one of the tenants of Ruskin's Guild of St. George cottages in Barmouth *(see pages 29 and 51)*. Born in Frotey-lès-Vesoul in the centre of France, he was a philanthropist and experimenter, and tried to establish a model community of his own in his home town. He described his experiments and hard work, which lasted 2 years, in his book, 'Lettres aux Gens de Frotey'. Although his scheme achieved much good for the less privileged, the local priests and Roman Catholic Church disliked his

Hen Blas public house with Ruskin's cottages in the background, c1875

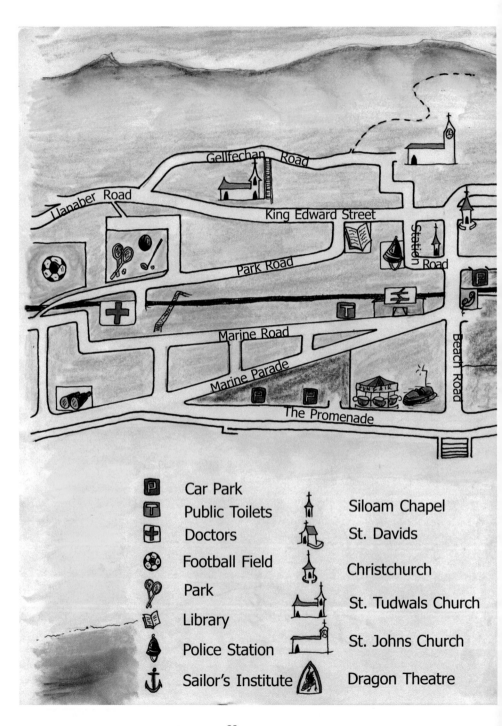

P	Car Park		
T	Public Toilets	Siloam Chapel	
+	Doctors	St. Davids	
⊕	Football Field	Christchurch	
	Park		
	Library	St. Tudwals Church	
	Police Station	St. Johns Church	
	Sailor's Institute	Dragon Theatre	

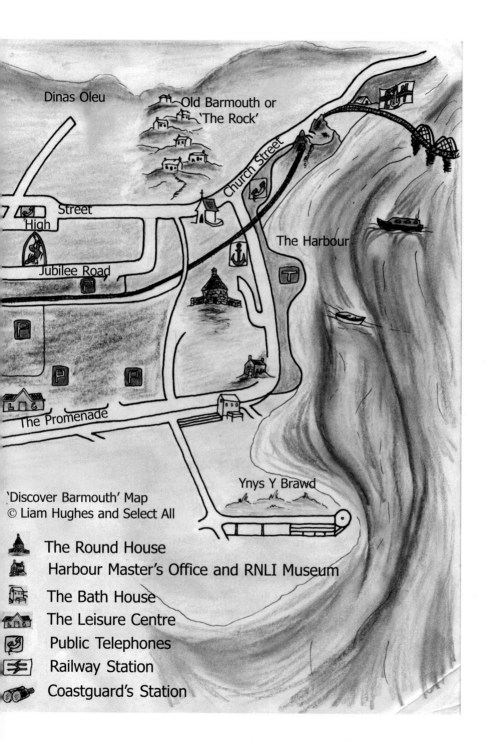

Dinas Oleu

Old Barmouth or 'The Rock'

Church Street

7 Street
'High

The Harbour

Jubilee Road

P

P

P   P

The Promenade

Ynys Y Brawd

'Discover Barmouth' Map
© Liam Hughes and Select All

The Round House

Harbour Master's Office and RNLI Museum

The Bath House

The Leisure Centre

Public Telephones

Railway Station

Coastguard's Station

methods and began to make life difficult for him. Eventually, he was forced to abandon his beloved scheme and escape to Paris. However, the war between France and Germany in 1870, and the seige of Paris made life even more uncomfortable for him.

One of M. Guyard's daughters lived in Barmouth, and was married to Quartus, son of Fanny Talbot. On hearing of M. Guyard's plight, Mrs. Talbot's kind nature came to the fore, and she offered him one of her cottages in Barmouth. He gratefully accepted, and moved to Wales with his other daughters.

Despite an almost complete lack of English - and of course Welsh - he quickly adapted himself to his new environment, and took great delight in helping his neighbours. He taught them how to cultivate vegetables on the terraced gardens of the rock. He educated them in the best herbs to grow for medicinal purposes and showed great kindness and skill when any of them were sick. When Ruskin visited Barmouth and the cottagers in 1876, he discovered in Guyard a kindred spirit and a model tenant for his project. In 1883, M. Auguste Guyard died. In accordance with his wishes, he was buried 150 feet above Tyn Y Ffynon, overlooking Barmouth rock and harbour. You can still visit his grave today *(see page 50)*, and you can also still see the walled remains of the terraced gardens that he diligently created on the ledges above Barmouth over 125 years ago.

Harold Godfrey Lowe (1883 - 1944)

Born to George and Emma Lowe of Penrallt, Barmouth, Harold Lowe, like many other Barmouth children, acquired a love for the sea from an early age. Whilst in his teens, his Father managed to secure him a valuable apprenticeship in Liverpool, Harold however ran away to sea. In 1912 he was appointed as 5th officer on the White Star Line's new boat, the Titanic. On the fateful evening of April 14, Lowe came off watch at around 10pm. By the time the ship hit the iceberg at 11.40pm, he was below deck, asleep in his quarters. On hearing voices and noises, and realising that something was amiss, he dressed and rushed up onto deck to help.

He was put in charge of lifeboat 14, the last but one to leave the port side. Altogether there were 58 persons on it, but only enough men for the oars. As the boat was being lowered into the sea, and passing one of the lower decks, men were clinging onto the rails, poised to jump into the boat.

Lowe drew his revolver and fired into the air. "That's just to show you that this pistol is loaded", he said to the men. "I'll kill anyone who attempts to get into this boat."

Unlike most of the other lifeboats, 14 was equipped with a small sail as well as oars. Once they were a safe distance from the sinking ship, Lowe took command of the situation, and joined his boat with 4 other fully laden ones that were rowing around aimlessly in the dark. He argued that 5 boats together would be easier to find.

Once the great ship had completely sunk into the Atlantic, the privileged minority in the lifeboats began to hear the cries of the majority struggling in the freezing water. Despite protests from the passengers, Lowe ordered that the people from lifeboat 14 should be transferred to the 4 other boats. He then took seamen Buley and Evans and lifeboat 14 with its sail, in search of survivors. His was the only boat to do so. After an hour of searching, he located only four survivors, one of which later died.

At 4.30am, five hours after Titanic hit the iceberg, the Carpathia arrived at the scene, and by 8.30am had collected 705 survivors from the lifeboats, the last of which was, quite literally, 5th Officer Lowe.

On June 21, 1912, in his home town of Barmouth, Harold Lowe was presented with a beautiful gold watch and chain, in recognition of his gallant services on the foundering of the Titanic.

He was soon promoted within the White Line service, and, being in the Royal Naval Reserve, he served as a Lieutenant in the Royal Navy during World War I. Little is known of his subsequent career. He died on May 12, 1944, aged 61,and was buried at Llandrillo-yn-Rhos Churchyard, Colwyn Bay.

Major Harold William Tilman (1898 - 1977).

Mountaineer, explorer, sailor and author, Bill Tilman was born in Wallasey, Cheshire, on 14th February, the son of a prosperous Liverpool merchant. In his late teens, he was determined to leave school and join the Army, and consequently passed the cadetship exam for the Royal Military Academy in November 1914. His service resulted in him fighting in both World Wars, winning medals  in each, including the Military Cross and the Victoria Cross.

In 1919 he left the army, and headed for Kenya. Ex-service applicants were being given a square mile of under developed land, but availability was limited and it was on a first come, first serve basis. Tilman was lucky. He ended up with a well-watered patch in a favourable location. Initially, his home was a tent on the land, but he then went on to construct and live in a series of mud huts, until he eventually found the time and money to construct a brick house. Initially, Tilman grew and harvested flax, but with a poor selling price, he moved onto growing coffee beans.

Tilman's life changed in 1930 when he read an article in a local newspaper regarding an Eric Shipton's ascent of Bation, one of Mount Kenya's twin peaks. He wrote to Shipton for advice on climbing. Shipton replied by offering to accompany Tilman on an expedition to Kilimanjaro in March 1930.

Kilimanjaro was to be the first of a series of travels and adventures across the world. Tilman went on to cycle across Africa (1933), make the first ascents of Midget Peak, Mt Kenya (1930), and Nanda Devi (1936), was a member of the 1935 Everest expedition, and led the 1938 attempt. After 1953 he sailed to Patagonia and crossed the ice cap, and completed the circumnavigation of South America and circumnavigated Africa (1957).

In 1947, Tilman moved to Glandwr, 2 miles east of Barmouth. His sister had recently bought 'Bod Owen', a comfortable house overlooking Mawddach estuary and the Cader range of mountains. Tilman loved the house and its view, and he lived there either planning his next expedition or writing his books.

He was an active member of the local community. In 1977 he became the first President of the Three Peaks Yacht Race *(see page 56)*, and, bearing in mind the race consists of sailing up the western coast of the British Isles and running up Snowdon, Scafell Pike and Ben Nevis, his vast experience was invaluable to the inaugural committee. He was also President of the Barmouth branch of the Royal National Lifeboat Institution.

In 1977 he planned an expedition to the Antarctic, where he hoped to spend his 80th birthday. Having left Southampton in early August, he reached Rio on 25 October. However, after leaving Rio, his vessel disappeared on route, and neither Tilman, or his boat, were ever seen again.

Other Notable Visitors

Like any other town, Barmouth has had its fair share of notable visitors over the years.

In 1812, Percy Shelley and his wife Harriet, travelled through the area in their search for a new home. When they were unable to find anything suitable, they hired an open boat, and continued south by sea for another 30 miles to Aberystwyth, and then onto Shelley's uncle's estate at Cwm Elan.

Another poet to visit the area, during 1823 to 1825, was William Wordsworth. Having rowed the length of the Mawddach estuary, he described it as 'sublime' and comparable with 'the finest in Scotland'.

Charles Darwin first came to the Barmouth area in 1828. He described in a letter to a friend of how he had discovered in the vicinity some of the rarest British insects. Over the years he kept returning, and was able to combine his research with his explorations of the locality. In 1869, following some of his greatest expeditions across the world in his boat, the Beagle, he came with his family to Caerdeon, about 3 miles east of Barmouth. He stayed there for 7 weeks and revised the fifth edition of his 'Origin of Species' and wrote part of his 'Descent of Man'.

In 1839, Tennyson visited Barmouth during a tour of North Wales. He described it as a 'prettier place than Aberystwyth', with its 'flat sand shore… and close behind them huge crags and a long estuary.'

During a week's vacation in Barmouth in 1892, William Gladstone, then Prime Minister, declared that the scenery on the Dolgellau to Barmouth road was only bettered by the scenery on the return journey.

Lloyd George, being a native of Criccieth, was a frequent visitor to Barmouth. He opened the town's newly constructed sea defences and promenade in 1933.

As the area has developed into a sought after location for many large budget movies, yesterday's poets and politicians have been replaced by television and film stars. Over the last 10 years, some of the productions which were filmed in the local area include 'First Knight' starring Richard Gere and Sean Connery, 'Merlin' starring Sam Neal, Miranda Richardson and the late Sir John Gielgud, and, most recently, in 2001, 'Happy Now', starring Ioan Gruffudd.

Chapter 5
Barmouth Lifeboat & Maritime Museum

Prior to the establishment of the RNLI in 1824, Barmouth had its own maritime rescue service, which would seek to help drowning seamen and wrecked vessels in the area. Their boat was housed in the basement of Pen-Y-Cei, which today is, fittingly, the Maritime Museum and Harbour Master's office.

In 1828, Barmouth's first RNLI lifeboat station was opened. It was on the beach near the bridge. Their first lifeboat was a 26-foot Palmer type, and cost £56. It was non-self righting, rowed six oars and weighed only 18cwts. It remained in service until the 1850s, and in 1852 a committee of local people was formed to raise money for a new boat.

The town gratefully took delivery of their new lifeboat in 1853. At the time, the practice of naming vessels had not developed. That was to become common practice in later years.

In those days of the RNLI and maritime rescue, the crew had only oars and sails to help them get out to a stricken vessel or individual. Motorised lifeboats did not begin to be introduced to stations until 1904, but it wasn't until 1948 that they had completely replaced the oar and sail fleet.

In 1967, fast inflatable crafts were introduced to Barmouth station. Primarily for inshore use, they are able to respond quickly to situations that require rapid action, such as drifting inflatable dinghies, or swimmers. These small crafts, or I.L.B. as they are known, are housed opposite the Bath House and, with a requirement of only three crew, and their close proximity to the beach, they are indispensable.

One of the most memorable days in recent times for the local lifeboat station and Barmouth people was in November 1982, when the Prince and Pricess of Wales visited the town to name the new lifeboat. The fund for the boat had been launched in 1981, the year of the Royal wedding, with the money being donated by the friends and people of Wales. A service of hymns and prayers took place on the Harbour, with a dedication and blessing of the boat. The quayside was a mass of people straining to catch a glimpse of the Royal couple who, at the time, had only been married for around 15 months. It was appropriate that the new boat was named 'The Princess of Wales'.

Since the introduction of the RNLI station to Barmouth, the town has had ten boats, the latest being "Moira Barrie", which was brought into service in 1992. All lifeboats, and their crew, are on duty 24 hours a day, 365 days of the year. Apart from the boat's mechanic, the coxswain and the 2nd coxswain, the crew is voluntary and unpaid. A small contribution towards drying their clothes is their only financial reward for risking their lives during a rescue. Up until the year 2000, the crew has been involved in the saving of 522 lives.

Many from Barmouth station have been praised for their heroic efforts through written 'acknowledgements' and medals. To highlight one individual or incident would undermine the efforts of the rest. However, some of the awards and stories are featured in Barmouth's Maritime Museum. Situated on the harbour, and adjoining the Harbour Master's office, entry is free, but donations are gratefully received. This small but interesting museum is run voluntarily by the Ladies Lifeboat Guild, and its purpose is to help raise funds for the RNLI and its stations. The Ladies Guild also conduct fund-raising events, including dances, coffee mornings and a Flag Day in August. All of which generate much needed income for the Institution.

In 1996 the first lifeboatwoman joined the Barmouth station. It is a welcome sign of the times to note that women are taking on roles as part of the crew, as well as on the fund raising committee.

The Moira Barrie, Barmouth's Lifeboat in 2002.

Chapter 6
Today and Yesterday
Cors Y Gedol c1865 and 2002

St. Annes Mansions and
Richmond Court c1865 and 2002

Harbour taken from Dinas Oleu
c1870 and 2002

Kings Crescent and Toll house
pre 1904 and 2002

Marine Parade
c1880 and 2002

Bath House and the construction of St. Johns Church 1891 and 2002

Can you find the locations of these businesses and streets?

Chapter 7
Walks

Advice for walkers

We have chosen three local walks that are suitable for people of differing abilities. However, we would recommend that all walkers wear walking boots or strong shoes for these routes. Most of the walks will entail crossing farmland and open fields, so please keep dogs on a lead at all times. We have provided an estimated time to allow for each walk. It may be wise to inform somebody of where you are going and how long you will be, but a mobile phone is also useful in case of difficulties. Finally, do not forget a camera, binoculars and, as you are in Wales, a waterproof of some kind.

The Countryside Code says that you should enjoy the countryside and respect its life and work. Guard against all risk of fire. Leave gates as you find them. Keep your dogs under close control. Keep to public paths across farmland. Use gates and stiles to cross fences, hedges and walls. Leave livestock, crops and machinery alone. Take your litter home. Help to keep all water clean. Protect wildlife, plants and trees. Take special care on country roads. Make no unnecessary noise.

Walk 1 - Around Old Barmouth Town

Introduction – A short walk, mainly comprising an uphill section, which is steep in parts, followed by the walk back down via uneven stone cobbled steps. Because of this, the walk is not suitable for very small children, individuals with walking difficulties, or wheelchair or pushchair users. As some of the paths are steep, sensible shoes should be worn. The National Trust has erected small wooden plaques, featuring a green oak leaf and an arrow, on the path upwards. Be careful though, they are difficult to see, as they are small, old and beginning to fade.

Highlights – This walk will provide you with panoramic views of the town and Cardigan Bay by taking you to the foot of Dinas Oleu, and then up to the Frenchman's Grave. The route back down offers you the option of exploring old Barmouth, which is known locally as 'The Rock' or 'Hen Bermo'.

Duration – Allow around 20 minutes, longer if you wish to enjoy the views or take a picnic at the top.

Starting Point – Woolworth's shop on Barmouth High Street.

Stage 1 – On the opposite side of the road to Woolworth and to the side of the Cors-Y-Gedol Hotel is a narrow unpaved road called Dinas Oleu Road which climbs up the hill to the back of Barmouth. Follow this road, over the crossroads that you pass almost immediately, and around a steep right hand bend. If you pause for a moment at this point, and turn around, you get an excellent view of the impressive St. Johns Church *(see page 27)*. Continuing onwards, you should then see one of the National Trust signs, where the road forks into two. As directed by the arrow on the sign, follow the right fork along the lower road.

Stage 2 – After approximately 200 metres, a grass path on the left-hand side, forks off the tarmac road and leads up the hill. Once again, a National Trust sign directs you along this route. The path is stoney and uneven in places, and there is a drop on the right hand side, so do not become too engrossed in the developing view.

Stage 3 – At the top of the path are two cottages. After passing the second cottage on the right, climb the set of stone steps located to the left-hand side. When you reach the top of the steps, you are at the foot of Dinas Oleu, which is owned by the National Trust. An information board explains the origins of the Trust and Dinas Oleu's former owner, Fanny Talbot *(see page 30)*. The cream coloured house behind you is on the site of Fanny Talbot's home, which was burned down in 1961. You will also be rewarded with a splendid view of Barmouth town, the harbour and Cardigan Bay.

Stage 4 – Carry on up the hillside following the path alongside Tyn y Ffynnon. At the top of the hill is a small metal gate. Continue through the gate and carry on upwards until you see a wooden gate on your right-hand side with the words 'Frenchman's Grave only' *(see page 30)* etched onto it. Pass through the gate and over the uneven path to the grave.

Stage 5 – After viewing the grave, head back down the hill to the gate and down to the path where the National Trust board stands. You now have a choice of two routes back down into the main town. The first is the path that heads back towards St. John's Church, which can be seen in the distance. If you follow this path, you will eventually rejoin your original route and come back to the starting point on the high street. The second choice provides more variety, and is via the old lanes and alleys of old Barmouth, known locally as The Rock. You can access this area by walking along the gravel path that borders the cream house. It will bring you to some steps that lead down to the maze of lanes between the cottages. It would be an impossible task to try and detail a particular route through this network of lanes, steps and alleys. It is far more interesting to discover your own, and as long as you keep heading downwards, you will eventually arrive back at the harbour

or the high street. On your descent, some points to look out for are Ruskin's cottages, the flagstone bridges that provide access to the upper floors of some cottages, and Auguste Guyard's terraced gardens, which are particularly noticeable on the upper reaches of the rock. Whichever path you decide to take, you are sure to discover some of the charm and flavour of the old town.

Walk 2 - Mountain Walk behind Barmouth

Introduction – This is a fairly energetic walk of around 2 to 3 miles. The first few stages consist of some steep uphill sections to reach the plateau of the hill. The latter stages bring you down, once again, via some steep roads into the eastern end of Barmouth. The walk is not suitable for individuals with walking difficulties, wheelchair or pushchair users, or young children.

Highlights – This walk explores the mountain area to the back of Barmouth, and will provide uninterrupted views of Cardigan Bay and the Lleyn Peninsula, the Mawddach Estuary, Cader Idris and Barmouth Bridge. You will also discover some of the area's heritage, including the old Drover's road, disused magnesium mines and derelict farms.

Duration – Allow between 2 and 3 hours, depending on your pace and stamina.

Starting Point – Spar on King Edward Street.

Stage 1 – Opposite Spar is a narrow road to the side of Hudson Estate Agents. Follow this road upward towards St. John's Church *(see page 27)*. As you approach the Church the road splits into a T-Junction. The right turn takes you alongside the imposing Church. However, we want to take Gellfechan Road to the left, which climbs (very) steeply around the back of St. John's Flats.

Stage 2 – The top of the steep section of hill is an appropriate point to regain your breath whilst admiring the panoramic view of the town and bay. Once rested, follow the public footpath sign down the grass track. This track leads you above and behind St. John's Church, providing you with a seagull's view of the tower and clock. As you continue, you will notice a number of caves that were formerly mined for their magnesium ore. One of the caves is known as the dripping well, providing some indication as to how wet they are, as well as unused and dangerous. At the end of the track you pass through an iron gate.

Stage 3 - At this point, the path divides once again. We want to turn left and head uphill. The route meanders quite steeply across the grassland and, after a few turns, it once again forks into two. Again, follow the left fork up the hill, eventually you will reach a metal gate. On the other side you will find the stone ruins of a number of buildings that used to be Gellfechan farm.

Stage 4 – As you leave the ruins, the path forks each side of a stone wall. Follow the path upward to the right, along the stone wall. At this point you

may notice a hill to your left with a pile of stones at the summit, which is known locally as The Peak or The Birmingham Memorial. After a while, you come to a gully. The path veers to the right and follows the gully upstream. This section appears to be part of the old drover's road.

Continuing through a wooden gate, you initially walk around a cluster of reeds and marshland on your left-hand side, until you find the relatively dry path through them to the slate bridge over a brook, and the metal gate in the stone wall.

Stage 5 – Once through the gate, the path continues alongside a wire fence. Continue to follow the path around the fenced field as it leads you in front of an isolated cottage (Gellfawr Farm) and onto the gravel track. You cross a small stream and after a short while the track leads you to a gate and stile. Once over the stile, you will notice on your right a public footpath sign and another stile, which lead across the field. Ignore these, and continue along the track.

Stage 6 – As the track reaches the brow of a small hill, an impressive panoramic view opens up to greet you. To your left/south, across the estuary, rises the Cader Idris range of mountains. Stretched out below you, meandering from east to west, is the Mawddach estuary, and to your right, Barmouth Bridge spans the mouth of estuary. You will also notice the large stone slabs on your right hand side, which are used for abseiling by the local outdoor pursuit centres.

Stage 7 – Continue along the tarmac road which joins Panorama Road. If you turn right onto this road and carry on downwards, you will eventually find yourself at the eastern end of Barmouth, by Porkington Terrace. A closer view of Barmouth Bridge and the lifeboat can be seen from the roadside as you make your way back into the town centre.

Walk 3 - Barmouth Bridge to Penmaenpool along the Mawddach Trail

Introduction – This is a six and a half mile walk across Barmouth Bridge and along the bed of the old railway track from Morfa Mawddach to Penmaenpool. The surface is flat with no hills, and the bridge section is suitable for wheelchair and pushchair users. The bed of the railway track however can be uneven in places, so individuals who are unsteady on their feet may find it difficult and, of course, it may be too long for young children. Dress warmly, as the bridge section can be windy and cold.

As this walk ends in Morfa Mawddach or Penmaenpool, we suggest you check the local train or bus timetables for the return journey to Barmouth. At certain times of year, services can be infrequent. You can also cycle along this route. It is usually possible to hire bicycles in Barmouth. The Tourist Information Centre can provide more details.

Highlights – This walk provides unparalleled views of the estuary, particularly whilst crossing the bridge. The railway track section provides some interesting diversions and plenty of nature of both plant and animal variety.

Duration – One way, allow around 3 hours, longer if you wish to make use of the picnic tables on route.

Starting Point – The Last Inn on the harbour

Stage 1 – From the pub, walk alongside the road as if you are heading out of Barmouth in the direction of Dolgellau. The road and pavement meander and climb between two large rocks. Immediately after the rocks you will see two openings on your right hand side. Go through the second opening. However, be careful crossing as the road is very narrow, visibility is poor and there is no pavement on the right hand side of the road. Once safely across, the opening leads you onto a path and down to the toll onto Barmouth Bridge. As is the nature of tolls, there is a small charge for crossing the bridge by foot or bicycle.

Stage 2 – Completed in 1867, the bridge is 2,292 feet long *(see page 20)*, and, although this section of the walk across the bridge can be windy and cold, the incomparable views along the estuary and out to sea make it worthwhile. Look out for cormorants, herons and oystercatchers on the sandbanks below the bridge. Once at the end of the bridge, follow the path through the gate and alongside the track to a small station called Morfa Mawddach. In the station's car park is a telephone and a public toilet (the only one on the walk!). From here, you could turn around and walk back over the bridge, or catch a train from the station (wave to get the driver to stop!). Energetic walkers however can continue along the former railway line alongside the estuary. To do so, continue to the end of the car park. As you pass the toilets, keep to the left, past a board with details of the Mawddach Trail, and then walk along a short wooded path. Soon you will cross a single lane road and pass through another gate and onto the main section of the trail.

Stage 3 – The route from here onwards simply follows the former railway line from Morfa Mawddach to Dolgellau. The actual rail route was closed on 18 January 1965, and the present day path is part of the National Cycle Network, 'Lon Las Cymru'. Funding from the European Community helps to maintain it. Along the walk there are other trails to divert you, including an RSPB Nature Reserve at Arthog Bog. Consisting of 12 acres of willow, alder scrub and flower rich grassland, this additional walk takes just under an hour.

Continuing along the estuary, you will find information boards detailing some of the points of interest around you, including the local wildlife and the heritage along the banks of the Mawddach. Eventually, the trail leads to the hamlet of Penmaenpool and it's toll bridge *(see page 13)*. For some, the most welcome sight will be the George III hotel, from where you can rest your feet and enjoy a beverage of your choice. Part of the hotel was originally the railway station, but was converted to accommodation when the line closed. Today, the former station's signal box is home to an RSPB observation point, which is usually open from Easter to October.

You now have the choice of either crossing the Penmaenpool Toll Bridge to catch a bus back to Barmouth, continue along the disused railway line to Dolgellau (approximately 3 more miles), or walk back along the same route to Barmouth.

There are, of course, many other walks in and around the Barmouth area. Barmouth book shops and the Tourist Information Centre should have leaflets and books suggesting other routes.

Chapter 8
Events and Festivals

Details of these events are for general guidance only. We would advise you to contact Barmouth's Tourist Information Centre on 01341 280787 prior to making any arrangements, as the dates and details are subject to change from year to year.

The Three Peaks Yacht Race

The first of a series of similar races around the world, the Barmouth to Fort William Three Peaks Yacht Race was started in 1977 by two local doctors, Dr. Rob Howarth and Dr. Merfyn Jones. When they dreamt up the initial idea they approached local mountaineer and sailor, the late Bill Tilman *(see page 35)*, for advice. He was so enthusiastic he became the event's first President.

The race consists of a team of five individuals sailing from Barmouth to Fort William, stopping on the way for two members of the team to run up three mountains, namely Snowdon, Scafell Pike and Ben Nevis. As if that challenge was not enough, in the year 2000 the organisers added a cycle stage at Whitehaven.

In summary, the event now consists of sailing 389 miles, running 59.5 miles, climbing 14,500 feet and cycling 26 miles. The current record for completing the event stands at 2 days and 9 hours.

The event normally takes place in June (tides have a bearing on the final date), and the boats usually start from Barmouth harbour at around midday.

Barmouth Jazz Festival

Launched in 2002, this is the latest event to be added to Barmouth's busy calendar of festivals. This ticket event will feature a select billing of some of Britain's finest jazz and blues musicians and is likely to be held in late May

Barmouth Music Festival

This weekend event started in 1997, and normally takes place in July. Each year the festival goes from strength to strength, its aim being to provide free music and family entertainment in and around Barmouth town. Past years have featured live acts from around the nation performing a diverse range of music including country and western, jazz, salsa, rock and Celtic folk. The town usually hosts two open-air stages, as well as live music in the pubs and around the town. For further information contact the festival office on 01341 281112.

Barmouth Harbour Festival & Annual Seven Mile Hill Run

The Harbour Festival rose from the smouldering remains of Barmouth Regatta, and includes many similar events and ideals, i.e. to provide fun and entertainment for all the family. Performers, clowns, competitions and live music is the entertainment around the harbour area over two weekends in August. Most of the events are free. The highlight of the whole festival is a large firework display that normally takes place on the Saturday evening of the last weekend.

The Seven Mile Hill Run is also held during the Harbour Festival, and involves running up the mountain at the back of Barmouth. Not for the faint hearted or the physically inactive. Fortunately, watching it can be just as entertaining.

Barmouth Arts Festival

Held in early September, this is one of Barmouth's longest established festivals. The week long event is usually host to, what some may regard as, the more refined and choice arts, such as classical music and theatre.

Barmouth Motocross Weekend

Launched in 2000, this exciting event is rapidly attracting a large group of followers. Specially prepared racecourses are created on Barmouth beach for this event, which usually takes place in early November. The semi-professional motorcycle and quad bike racers, who gather in the town for the event, provide an endless amount of thrills and spills. The beach and promenade are perfect hosts for this adrenaline-pumping event. The organisers often combine the weekend with a bonfire and fireworks display on the Saturday evening.

Chapter 9
Local Stories and Rumours

The Battle of the Barmouth Boys

During the Second World War, Barmouth and other local villages, such as Llwyngwril and Arthog, became an important training area for the Marine Naval Base Defence Organisation II. Their camps in the locality were used to train troops in seamanship, and for preparations for the D-Day landing operations. Over the course of the war years the area became a hive of military activity.

One Thursday, in the summer of February 1944, three thirteen-year-old Barmouth boys broke into the armoury in Barmouth town. Although the building was guarded, the boys waited until a change in the guard took place and then climbed in though an open window! Differing versions of the story exist, but supposedly they stole three rifles and between 400 and 5,000 rounds of ammunition. The boys then took to the hills behind Barmouth with their weapons and began shooting at the local wildlife. The locals in the town began to panic that German paratroopers had landed, and when the theft from the armoury was discovered, the Lieutenant-quartermaster was recalled from leave and the brigadier's batman was sent to try and catch the culprits. With the boys strategically entrenched on higher ground, successive attempts by the regimental police, the National Fire Service and a platoon of 36 marines failed, as rounds began to be fired above their heads.

The 'battle' continued for 2 days and 2 nights and involved around 2,000 troops searching the hills for the boys. Eventually, the fugitives ran out of ammunition and were forced to surrender from their position in one of the area's disused mines.

At the time, the military and the authorities were naturally embarrassed by the incident, and were keen to keep the details under wraps. Allegedly, there were rumours of Churchill wanting the boys prosecuted for attempted murder. However, following an appearance at Barmouth Juvenile Court, they were sent to an approved school.

In recent years the story has come back into focus following revelations that a television company are planning to use the incident as the basis for a film. However, filming will take place in Yorkshire and, in the interest of television entertainment, details of the actual event have supposedly been dramatically revised.

The Haunting at the Lion Inn

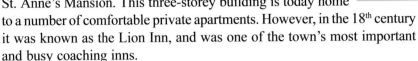

Next to the R.A.O.B. club, and behind the Carousel café, stands St. Anne's Mansion. This three-storey building is today home to a number of comfortable private apartments. However, in the 18th century it was known as the Lion Inn, and was one of the town's most important and busy coaching inns.

One evening, towards the end of the 18th century, a wealthy jeweller arrived at the inn on his beautiful white horse. Together with his servant they were booked into rooms on the top floor of the Inn for that night.

By mid-morning of the following day, the landlord and his wife became concerned when the jeweller had not made an appearance. On further investigation, he did not reply to their calls and the door to his room was locked fast. Eventually, they managed to force entry and, to their horror, discovered the jeweller lying in a pool of blood on the bedroom floor. He had been murdered. They quickly searched the rest of the Inn, but could find no trace of the jeweller's servant, the jeweller's treasures or his magnificent white horse. Despite extensive enquiries by the Police and authorities, the servant was never caught or convicted.

A few weeks later, some guests at the Inn began complaining of hearing strange noises that seemed to emanate from the jeweller's former room. Stranger still, some also claimed to hear horses hooves galloping across the roof. The stories continued and the landlord's business began to suffer as staff reported seeing a white apparition of a horse on the roof and a ghostly face in the circular window at the top of the Inn.

Eventually, the Vicar of Pwllheli was called in to "lay the ghost to rest". Reverend Williams was renowned locally for the powers he possessed over the spirits of darkness. Presumably, he achieved the difficult feat he was set, as no other ghostly experiences were reported…apart from the bloodstains on the floor boards, which allegedly have never been erased.

The Bathing Machines *(see photo on page 15)*

The following is taken from the Barmouth Advertiser of July 26, 1883, which, in turn, quotes extracts from the Guardian of October 18, 1882.

'The bathing customs are in some respects refreshingly primitive. Advancing civilisation has, it is true, effected a separation between the ladies and the gentlemen's machines – at the request, it is said, of the stronger sex; and an enigmatically worded notice enacts that "No male person of twelve years old and upwards shall bathe within 100 yards of the ladies' machines, and shall wear drawers." But beyond this limit bathing goes on freely from the shore; the process of getting out of ordinary dress and into the said drawers being performed *sub divo* under the eyes of the ladies, who in some cases sit by and guard their husbands' clothes. I have also seen before breakfast a lady enveloped in an ulster walk down to a conspicuous part of the beach, and there let fall the ulster, disclosing a bathing-dress in which she walked straight into the sea – My breakfast was ready, or curiosity would have led me to wait and see whether on coming out she simply replaced the ulster on her dripping form, or whether by some sleight of body she contrived to wriggle out of her wet robes into its protecting folds and walked home in that alone. I am inclined to believe the latter alternative; for I have noticed ladies going towards their machines carrying their bathing-gowns and shrouded in ulsters which obviously concealed little or nothing but the wearer herself. On Sunday mornings the machines are not drawn down to the water, but may be used by bathers."

Was there a Barmy in Barmouth?

Sightings of mysterious sea creatures in the Cardigan Bay area have been documented since 1937. In that year, a Mr. Jones of Harlech observed 'a crocodile-like creature' walking beside a local riverbank. However, the rumours and stories really started to gather pace in the 1970s, when a series of incidents were documented by the local and national press.

The first incident came from the Menai Straits area, to the north of Barmouth, in the early 70s, and was reported by four fishermen. They claimed to have seen a creature about 10 feet long raise itself out of the water near the kelpie beds, and then submerge and disappear. Their description seemed to match one of the most famous sightings, which was made by six schoolgirls from Barmouth. In broad daylight, on 2nd March 1975, the girls claimed to have seen an animal that "had a long neck, and a square face, and a long tail with a flipper at the back, and its skin was black and patchy." Their art teacher was so convinced by their account that he produced a postcard giving an artist's impression of what they saw. Over the next few years the frequency of the sightings increased, and the monster was christened 'Barmy' by the local press. In 1975, a couple on a yachting holiday claimed to have encountered an unidentified sea animal with "double sharply pointed spines" five miles off the coast of Harlech.

They further described the creature as having "a free-moving neck, fairly short, rather like a turtle's, and an egg-shaped head about the size of a seals. Its back had two spines, which were sharply ridged, and it was about eight feet across and eleven feet long."

A year later, 2 people, who were staying in a caravan park at Talybont, claimed to have found on the beach one morning the bodies of six 'monsters'. They described them as having long necks, small heads, and bodies supported at the rear by two legs. There was also an anonymous report of large footprints 'as big as elephants' on Barmouth beach, and a bather who found herself within touching distance of what appeared to be a sea monster. She swam to shore as fast as she could.

One sighting, which is more difficult to dismiss, occurred in August 1976. In a signed statement, a Gwent Solicitor and his son documented how they were drying themselves following an early morning dip by Barmouth's causeway. Suddenly, their attention was drawn by a "dark brown solid object", about 10 feet in length, which seemed to be causing a disturbance in the water. Initially, it was around 100 yards away from them, but after the fifth disturbance, it was a mile away. They were puzzled by the speed of the object, and at a loss to identify it.

Over the years, other sightings of mysterious creatures aand discturbances were reported. The vast majority seemed to come from visitors oblivious to previous incidents.

However, in 1988 it seemed that the mystery had been solved. On September 22nd of that year, a leather-backed turtle was washed up onto Harlech beach. Measuring eight feet wide and eight feet in length, it weighed 2,016 lbs., and, to date, is the largest leather-backed turtle ever recorded in the world. At the time, it was thought to have come from the Caribbean or North Africa, and was probably attracted to the area by the large number of jellyfish. The zoology department of the National Museum of Wales took the turtle away for examination.

Was this enormous turtle the same as the one encountered by visitors and locals, or, was it just one of many different and mysterious creatures that roam the waters of Cardigan Bay?

Chapter 10
Welsh Words & Place Names

Useful Phrases

Please – Oes Gwelwch Chi'n Dda
Thank You – Diolch
Good Morning – Bore Da
Good Night – Nos Da
How are you? – Sut Ydych Chi?

Words used in local place names

Aber –mouth of a river
Betws – a house of prayer
Bont –bridge
Cadair –chair
Coed – a wood
Castell – castle
Cwm – a small valley
Dinas – fort, city
Dyffryn - valley
Eglwys - church
Felin – mill
Hendre – winter dwelling

Mynach - monk
Llech – slate
Llyn – lake or pool
Moel – bare hill
Mynydd – mountain
Plas - mansion
Penmaen – rocky headland
Pentre - village
Rhadear – waterfall
Traws – across.
Ynys – island

Place Names

Abermawddach – at the mouth of the river mawddach
Bontddu – blackbridge
Betws-Y-Coed – prayer house in the woods
Coed-Y-Brenin – King's wood.
Pwllheli – saltwater pool
Tal-y-bont – end of the bridge
Tywyn – sandy plain near a seashore
Trawsfynydd – across a mountain

Barmouth - Useful Information

CASH POINTS – Barclays, Natwest, HSBC and Link at the Co-operative supermarket.

DOCTORS – Minfor Surgery, Park Road, tel. - 01341 280521. Out of hours tel. - 01286 674421.

GOLF – Dolgellau (10 miles inland), Harlech (10 miles north).

HALF DAY CLOSING – Wednesday, although most shops stay open during the season.

HARBOUR MASTERS – situated on the quay, tel. - 01341 280671.

LEISURE CENTRE – situated on the promenade, tel. - 01341 280111.

LIBRARY – on Talbot square, Station Road. Internet access available on booking. Tel. - 01341 280258.

MARKET – Thursdays (and Sundays during season only) on the car park next to Woolworth.

POLICE STATION – opposite railway station. Tel. - 01341 280222.

POST OFFICE - NBS Ltd, High Street. Tel. - 01341 280534

RECREATION GROUND - Tennis, Bowls, Putting Green and Children's Playground situated on Park Road opposite footbridge.

SEA FISHING - Various trips available from Harbour.

SWIMMING POOLS – Porthmadog Leisure Centre (20 miles north). Tywyn Swimming Pool (25 miles south). Machynlleth Leisure Centre (28 miles east). Harlech Swimming Pool (10 miles north).

TOURIST INFORMATION - Station road open Easter to October. Tel. - 01341 280787.